BIRD VIEWING AREAS

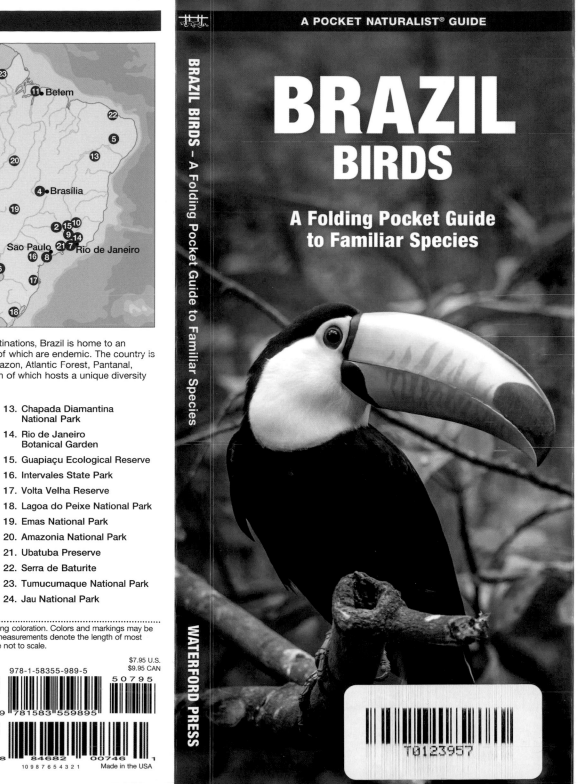

One of the world's prime birding destinations, Brazil is home to an incredible 1,800+ species, over 200 of which are endemic. The country is divided into six natural regions – Amazon, Atlantic Forest, Pantanal, Cerrado, Pampa and Caatinga – each of which hosts a unique diversity of species.

1. Pantanal Biosphere Reserve
2. Serra da Canastra National Park
3. Presidente Figueiredo
4. Brasilia National Park
5. Caatinga Biosphere Reserve
6. Iguazu Falls
7. National Museum of Brazil
8. Museum of Zoology of the University of São Paulo
9. Itatiaia National Park
10. Rio Doce State Park
11. Museu Paraense Emílio Goeldi
12. Pico da Neblina National Park
13. Chapada Diamantina National Park
14. Rio de Janeiro Botanical Garden
15. Guapiaçu Ecological Reserve
16. Intervales State Park
17. Volta Velha Reserve
18. Lagoa do Peixe National Park
19. Emas National Park
20. Amazonia National Park
21. Ubatuba Preserve
22. Serra de Baturite
23. Tumucumaque National Park
24. Jau National Park

Most illustrations show the adult male in breeding coloration. Colors and markings may be duller or absent during different seasons. The measurements denote the length of most animals from nose/bill to tail tip. Illustrations are not to scale.

Waterford Press publishes reference guides to nature observation, outdoor recreation and survival skills. Product information is featured on the website:
www.waterfordpress.com

Text & illustrations © 2016, 2023 Waterford Press Inc. All rights reserved. Photos © Shutterstock. To order or for information on custom published products please call 800-434-2555 or email orderdesk@waterfordpress.com. For permissions or to share comments email editor@waterfordpress.com. 2301408

$7.95 U.S.
$9.95 CAN

ISBN 978-1-58355-989-5
9 781583 559895
50795

UPC 8 84682 00740 1
10987654321
Made in the USA

A POCKET NATURALIST® GUIDE

BRAZIL
BIRDS

A Folding Pocket Guide to Familiar Species

BRAZIL BIRDS – A Folding Pocket Guide to Familiar Species

WATERFORD PRESS

T0123957

WATERBIRDS & NEARSHORE BIRDS

Fulvous Whistling-Duck
Dendrocygna bicolor To 20 in. (50 cm)
Tawny duck has a white side stripe.

Least Grebe
Tachybaptus dominicus To 10 in. (25 cm)

Magellanic Penguin
Spheniscus magellanicus To 30 in. (75 cm)
Has a braying call and is also called the jackass penguin.

Black-bellied Whistling-Duck
Dendrocygna autumnalis To 21 in. (53 cm)

Pied-billed Grebe
Podilymbus podiceps To 13 in. (33 cm)
Note banded white bill.

Masked Duck
Nomonyx dominicus To 13 in. (33 cm)

Muscovy Duck
Cairina moschata To 32 in. (80 cm)
Face is "warty".

Brazilian Teal
Amazonetta brasiliensis To 16 in. (40 cm)

Horned Screamer
Anhima cornuta To 38 in. (95 cm)
Wetland bird is named for it's loud, screaming calls.

Ruddy Turnstone
Arenaria interpres To 10 in. (25 cm)

Spotted Sandpiper
Actitis macularius To 8 in. (20 cm)
Breast is spotted.

Red Knot
Calidris canutus To 12 in. (30 cm)

White-faced Whistling-Duck
Dendrocygna viduata To 18 in. (45 cm)

Greater Yellowlegs
Tringa melanoleuca To 15 in. (38 cm)
Call is a 3-5 note whistle.

American Oystercatcher
Haematopus palliatus To 20 in. (50 cm)

Lesser Yellowlegs
Tringa flavipes To 10 in. (25 cm)
Call is a 1-3 note whistle.

WATERBIRDS & NEARSHORE BIRDS

Sunbittern
Eurypyga helias To 18 in. (45 cm)

Southern Lapwing
Vanellus chilensis To 15 in. (38 cm)

Collared Plover
Charadrius collaris To 6 in. (15 cm)

South American Snipe
Gallinago paraguaiae To 12 in. (30 cm)

Sanderling
Calidris alba To 8 in. (20 cm)
Runs in and out with waves along shorelines.
Winter

Rufous-sided Crake
Laterallus melanophaius To 6 in. (15 cm)

Purple Gallinule
Porphyrio martinicus To 13 in. (33 cm)

Neotropic Cormorant
Phalacrocorax brasilianus To 26 in. (65 cm)

Common Gallinule
Gallinula chloropus To 14 in. (35 cm)

Large-billed Tern
Phaetusa simplex To 16 in. (40 cm)

Wattled Jacana
Jacana jacana To 9 in. (23 cm)

Gray-necked Wood-rail
Aramides cajanea To 16 in. (40 cm)

Black Skimmer
Rynchops niger To 20 in. (50 cm)
Feeds by skimming over water with its lower bill cutting the water's surface to spear fish.

Sandwich Tern
Thalasseus sandvicensis To 18 in. (45 cm)
Black bill has a yellow tip.

Kelp Gull
Larus dominicanus To 23 in. (58 cm)
Note all-white tail.

WATERBIRDS & NEARSHORE BIRDS

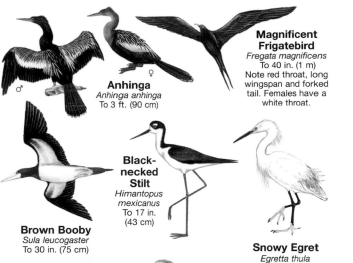

Anhinga
Anhinga anhinga To 3 ft. (90 cm)

Magnificent Frigatebird
Fregata magnificens To 40 in. (1 m)
Note red throat, long wingspan and forked tail. Females have a white throat.

Black-necked Stilt
Himantopus mexicanus To 17 in. (43 cm)

Brown Booby
Sula leucogaster To 30 in. (75 cm)

Snowy Egret
Egretta thula To 26 in. (65 cm)
Note black bill and yellow feet.

Jabiru
Jabiru mycteria To 55 in. (1.4 m)

Cattle Egret
Bubulcus ibis To 20 in. (50 cm)

Wood Stork
Mycteria americana To 4 ft. (1.2 m)
Dark head is naked.

Great Egret
Ardea alba To 38 in. (95 cm)
Note yellow bill and black feet.

Striated Heron
Butorides striatus To 14 in. (35 cm)
Note black cap.

Cocoi Heron
Ardea cocoi To 43 in. (1.1 m)
Note white neck.

Flamingo
Phoenicopterus spp.
To 4 ft. (1.2 m)
Found near brackish lakes and lagoons.

Rufescent Tiger-Heron
Tigrisoma lineatum To 28 in. (70 cm)

Boat-billed Heron
Cochlearius cochlearius To 21 in. (53 cm)

WATERBIRDS & NEARSHORE BIRDS

Scarlet Ibis
Eudocimus ruber To 25 in. (63 cm)

Buff-necked Ibis
Theristicus caudatus To 27 in. (68 cm)

Roseate Spoonbill
Platalea ajaja To 32 in. (80 cm)
Bill is flattened at the tip.

DOVES, CUCKOOS, ETC.

Rock Pigeon
Columba livia To 13 in. (33 cm)

Gray-fronted Dove
Leptotila rufaxilla To 12 in. (30 cm)

Ruddy Ground-dove
Columbina talpacoti To 6 in. (15 cm)

Eared Dove
Zenaida auriculata To 10 in. (25 cm)

Squirrel Cuckoo
Piaya cayana To 20 in. (50 cm)

Guira Cuckoo
Guira guira To 14 in. (35 cm)

Dusky-legged Guan
Penelope obscura To 28 in. (70 cm)

Great Tinamou
Tinamus major To 18 in. (45 cm)
One of several similar species.

Black Curassow
Crax alector To 38 in. (95 cm)

Greater Rhea
Rhea americana To 56 in. (1.4 m)
Note large size.

Hoatzin
Opisthocomus hoazin To 26 in. (65 cm)
Also known as "stinkbird", it has a manure-like odor.

PARROTS, TOUCANS, ETC.

Blue-and-Yellow Macaw
Ara ararauna
To 34 in. (85 cm)

Red-and-Green Macaw
Ara chloropterus
To 38 in. (95 cm)

Scarlet Macaw
Ara macao
To 34 in. (85 cm)

Hyacinth Macaw
Anodorhynchus hyacinthinus
To 40 in. (1 m)

White-eyed Parakeet
Aratinga leucophthalma
To 13 in. (33 cm)

Peach-fronted Parakeet
Aratinga aurea
To 10 in. (25 cm)

Blue-headed Parrot
Pionus menstruus
To 11 in. (28 cm)

Common Potoo
Nyctibius griseus
To 15 in. (38 cm)

Orange-winged Parrot
Amazona amazonica
To 12 in. (30 cm)

Green Kingfisher
Chloroceryle americana
To 8 in. (20 cm)
The similar Amazon kingfisher is larger.

Ringed Kingfisher
Megaceryle torquata
To 14 in. (35 cm)

Amazon Kingfisher
Chloroceryle amazona
To 12 in. (30 cm)

White-throated Toucan
Ramphastos tucanus
To 2 ft. (60 cm)

Channel-billed Toucan
Ramphastos vitellinus
To 25 in. (62 cm)

Black-necked Aracari
Pteroglossus aracari
To 18 in. (45 cm)

Toco Toucan
Ramphastos toco
To 24 in. (60 cm)

Chestnut-eared Aracari
Pteroglossus castanotis
To 18 in. (45 cm)

TROGONS, WOODPECKERS ETC.

Green-backed Trogon
Trogon viridis
To 12 in. (30 cm)

Surucua Trogon
Trogon surrucura
To 10 in. (25 cm)

Blue-crowned Trogon
Trogon curucui
To 10 in. (25 cm)

Black-throated Trogon
Trogon rufus
To 9 in. (23 cm)

Glittering-throated Emerald
Amazila fimbriata
To 4 in. (10 cm)

Plantano Hermit
Phaethornis pretrei
To 5 in. (13 cm)

Black-throated Mango
Anthracothorax nigricollis
To 5 in. (13 cm)

Glittering-bellied Emerald
Chlorostilbon lucidus
To 4 in. (10 cm)

Swallow-tailed Hummingbird
Eupetomena macroura
To 6 in. (15 cm)

Amethyst Woodstar
Calliphlox amethystina
To 3 in. (8 cm)

Rufous-tailed Jacamar
Galbula ruficauda
To 9 in. (23 cm)

Smooth-billed Ani
Crotophaga ani
To 12 in. (30 cm)

Campo Flicker
Colaptes campestris
To 12 in. (30 cm)

Lineated Woodpecker
Dryocopus lineatus
To 14 in. (35 cm)

Green-barred Woodpecker
Colaptes melanochloros
To 10 in. (25 cm)

Little Woodpecker
Veniliornis passerinus
To 6 in. (15 cm)

BIRDS OF PREY

Snail Kite
Rostrhamus sociabilis
To 19 in. (48 cm)
Feeds primarily on snails.

White-tailed Kite
Elanus leucurus
To 17 in. (43 cm)

Swallow-tailed Kite
Elanoides forficatus
To 2 ft. (60 cm)

Turkey Vulture
Cathartes aura
To 32 in. (80 cm)
Note two-toned underwings.

Black Vulture
Coragyps atratus
To 27 in. (68 cm)

Greater Yellow-headed Vulture
Cathartes melambrotus
To 5.5 ft. (1.7 m)

American Kestrel
Falco sparverius
To 12 in. (30 cm)

White-tailed Hawk
Geranoaetus albicaudatus
To 23 in. (58 cm)

Great Black Hawk
Buteogallus urubitinga
To 26 in. (65 cm)

Harpy Eagle
Harpia harpyja
To 40 in. (1 m)
The largest raptor in the Americas.

Yellow-headed Caracara
Milvago chimachima
To 18 in. (45 cm)

Osprey
Pandion haliaetus
To 2 ft. (60 cm)

Roadside Hawk
Buteo magnirostris
To 16 in. (40 cm)

Southern Caracara
Caracara plancus
To 25 in. (63 cm)

Burrowing Owl
Athene cunicularia
To 11 in. (28 cm)
Usually seen on the ground, it lives in underground burrows.

PERCHING BIRDS

White-winged Swallow
Tachycineta albiventer
To 5 in. (13 cm)

Blue-and-White Swallow
Notiochelidon cyanoleuca
To 5 in. (13 cm)

Southern Rough-winged Swallow
Stelgidopteryx ruficollis
To 5 in. (13 cm)

Barn Swallow
Hirundo rustica
To 8 in. (20 cm)
Note deeply forked tail.

Gray-breasted Martin
Progne chalybea
To 7 in. (18 cm)

White-winged Becard
Pachyramphus polychopterus
To 6 in. (15 cm)

Woodcreeper
Xiphorhynchus/ Dendrocolaptes/ Lepidocolaptes spp.
To 9 in. (23 cm)
Several similar species feed by probing for insects on tree trunks.

Amazonian Umbrellabird
Cephalopterus ornatus
To 22 in. (55 cm)

White-headed Marsh-tyrant
Arundinicola leucocephala
To 5 in. (13 cm)

Blue Manakin
Chiroxiphia caudata
To 6 in. (15 cm)

Common Tody-Flycatcher
Todirostrum cinereum
To 9 in. (23 cm)

Red-eyed Vireo
Vireo olivaceus
To 6 in. (15 cm)
Note gray crown and red eye.

Fork-tailed Flycatcher
Tyrannus savana
To 16 in. (40 cm)

White-naped Jay
Cyanocorax cyanopogon
To 14 in. (35 cm)

Tropical Kingbird
Tyrannus melancholicus
To 8 in. (20 cm)

PERCHING BIRDS

Epaulet Oriole
Icterus cayanensis
To 8 in. (20 cm)

Blue Dacnis
Dacnis cayana
To 5 in. (13 cm)

Purple-throated Euphonia
Euphonia chlorotica
To 4 in. (10 cm)

Rufous-bellied Thrush
Turdus rufiventris
To 10 in. (25 cm)
Brazil's National Bird.

Rufous Hornero
Furnarius rufus
To 8 in. (20 cm)

House Wren
Troglodytes aedon
To 5 in. (13 cm)

Green Honeycreeper
Chlorophanes spiza
To 5 in. (13 cm)

Red-legged Honeycreeper
Cyanerpes cyaneus
To 5 in. (13 cm)

Buff-throated Saltator
Saltator maximus
To 8 in. (20 cm)

Ultramarine Grosbeak
Cyanocompsa brissoni
To 6 in. (15 cm)

Red-capped Cardinal
Paroaria gularis
To 7 in. (18 cm)

Screaming Piha
Lipaugus vociferans
To 10 in. (25 cm)
Extraordinarily loud, explosive call – Wit-witjuh – is a common rainforest sound.

Bananaquit
Coereba flaveola
To 5 in. (13 cm)

Great Kiskadee
Pitangus sulphuratus
To 9 in. (23 cm)

Yellow-rumped Cacique
Cacicus cela
To 12 in. (30 cm)

PERCHING BIRDS

Hepatic Tanager
Piranga flava
To 8 in. (20 cm)

Paradise Tanager
Tangara chilensis
To 6 in. (15 cm)

Blue-gray Tanager
Thraupis episcopus
To 6 in. (15 cm)

Palm Tanager
Thaupis palmarum
To 7 in. (18 cm)

Silver-beaked Tanager
Ramphocelus carbo
To 7 in. (18 cm)

Burnished-buff Tanager
Tangara cayana
To 6 in. (15 cm)

Magpie Tanager
Cissopis leverianus
To 12 in. (30 cm)

Shiny Cowbird
Molothrus bonariensis
To 8 in. (20 cm)

Chestnut-capped Blackbird
Chrysomus ruficapillus
To 8 in. (20 cm)

Black-tailed Tityra
Tityra cayana
To 8 in. (20 cm)

Great Antshrike
Taraba major
To 8 in. (20 cm)

Chalk-browed Mockingbird
Mimus saturninus
To 10 in. (25 cm)

Saffron Finch
Sicalis flaveola
To 5 in. (13 cm)

Rufous-collared Sparrow
Zonotrichia capensis
To 6 in. (15 cm)

House Sparrow
Passer domesticus
To 6 in. (15 cm)